Inside, Outside, Morningside

poems

Inside, Outside, Morningside

poems

Marjorie Kowalski Cole

Ester Republic Press
Ester, Alaska

Inside, Outside, Morningside
© 2009 Marjorie Kowalski Cole. All rights reserved.

Published in Ester, Alaska
by the Ester Republic Press, PO Box 24, Ester AK, 99725 U.S.A.
www.esterrepublic.com • info@esterrepublic.com • 907.451.0636

Printed in the United States of America
by Thomson-Shore
an employee-owned company
member of the Green Press Initiative

author photo by Pat Lambert
photo of seiner by CP McRoy
design and production by Deirdre Helfferich

ISBN: 978-0-9749221-6-4 (paperback)

Library of Congress Control Number: 2009940491

My thanks to editors of these journals, where the following poems first appeared:

Alaska Quarterly Review: Henry's Nelson Coat

Antigonish Review: Dutch Interiors; A Heart that is Pleased by the Sea

Cirque: Water; Wildlife on Old Wood Road

The Ester Republic: Coming Up On Solstice; Eight-Sided Art; Ice Cream; Prom Night; Pushkin; Republican Sweep 2004; The Dog at the Top of the Road; The Top of the World from Inside Jeanie's Parka; Three Birch Trees, or Maybe Four; When the Bookmobile Comes to Ester, Alaska

Explorations: Mom and her Girlfriends, Miami Beach

Ginosko: Light and its Absence

Grain: A Poem in the Hand: Not Drinking Song

Ice Floe: Fire-filled Summer

National Catholic Reporter: Batman Next Door; If You Want a Drunkard; Mediterranean Evening

The Northern Review: Raspberry Canes Along the Fence

The Other Side: Codladh Sámh

Prism International: The Playing Field

Room of One's Own: Apple Wood; Desire; Inside, Outside, Morningside

Seattle Review: Siesta

Awards:

"A Heart that is Pleased by the Sea" received second place in the October 2000 *Glimmer Train* Poetry Open; "Mom and her Girlfriends, Miami Beach" received the 2000 *Explorations* Poetry Prize; "Coming Up on Solstice" and "Ice Cream" received the annual Publisher's Award from *The Ester Republic;* "Non" was a finalist in the 2007 Strokestown, Ireland, Poetry Festival.

Dedication

This book of poems is for my sons,
Henry L. Cole and Desmond R. Cole,
with all my love.

Poems

-|||-

THE WORK OF OUR HANDS

Desire

Desire

"The clamor made by machines and industry smothers the soft sounds of human desire…"
—Anthony Padovano, *The Human Journey*

What if I put words to it,
after all.
The way the field
puts on a light skin
of new snow, the way my hands
discover the shape of your face—
What if I put words to it:
said, your eyes are yellow,
like water through aspen leaves;
your eyes hold patience

as the wild creature in the grass
is patient; the hillside on which we stand
looking at one another
is patient,
spirit and skeleton
revealed at once in leafless stalks
· of highbush cranberry.
Under the porch a red squirrel
with a mushroom in its paws
provides against the cold.

The lushness of life falls back.
· In its absence I feel most strongly
a loveliness in the world
struggling to be born
again in consciousness.
The aspens shake in the wind
like the bells of a prayer wheel.
I would have what is within and without
arrive at one still moment
together.

Salty

I watched as you knocked the salt
off a pretzel. Rubbed it smooth
before you bit down. I wanted to say,
"but since they come that way..."

"Salt on the rim?" asked the bargirl
at the real Salty Dawg on the Homer Spit.
"No thanks!" you replied to my dismay.
I'd have gone after those crystals as after life itself.

Once a priest told us of a friend
who gave up salt for his health's sake.
"Can you imagine a life without salt, without savor?"
the priest pleaded; he had a point to make,

spoke more with fervor than wit
while you writhed at his ignorance:
doesn't know the first thing about modern medicine,
and the homily sent me off to images

of fried eggs under cracked pepper,
butter melting into grits. As for you and me,
perhaps we are not given a choice.
It does not do to deny the chemistry of pain.

The whore booked.
Your salty bitch moved on, though no one asked politely,
"Today will you have grief with no outlet
and become as bitter as a lake that kills?"

In the Russian fable the youngest son
brought salt home to the king; a crystal shaker
on the bishop's table comforts his loneliness,
impresses a guest. When you raised your head

from between my legs, I was among the stars.
Salt is our gift, an exchange glistening
on our skin. Part of the earth,
if you like, though it flows in our veins, and the sea.

The Playing Field

June in Fairbanks. Birch
and aspen explode, light green
bulging over the road. A cutbank
of silt, black pyramids of topsoil.
Two boys on a fourwheeler
leaving the gravel pit at ten pm.

The sun like an open stove
at this hour burns the eyes
of the woman leaving her husband.
Tears splash behind sunglasses.
Across town an eighth grader
learns to slide into third
covering new white pants
with dirt, oh the honor of it.

At midnight his newly single dad
rinses them in the bathtub
Everywhere hands plunge
into the earth. A robin cuts low
across the yard, sparrows forage
in blonde grass, a dog comes out of the woods
with two baby hares in her mouth,
lays them alive at her master's feet.
See what I found.

Prom Night

April evening in Fairbanks; a reading
on the top floor of the Civic Center.
In the hall below, students gather for the prom.
Excited by the conjunction the poet reads to us
about his junior prom, thirty years ago;
he glows with the memory of the rented tux
and borrowed Cadillac. Downstairs
my own son is arriving at this moment.
Turned down by three girls, he's going alone
in his father's jacket. His parents' divorce
fractured his own joy years ago,
gave him a real taste of fear.
But tonight, his priorities are clear.

Girls like the stems of iris
dressed in velvet and taffeta, red, black, ivory
shoulders pure as ice cream,
boys shining above white shirts, every head slick.
We are slumped on our spines at the reading
legs crossed John Singer Sargent style
wishing they still served wine at these things
but the children downstairs are like graceful pipes
legs barely opening as they glide.
At first girls dance with each other;
Boys hang together in corners, venture onto the floor
Late in the night. Their faces are moonbeams
as they offer themselves to the world.

The poet tells us that he runs eight miles a day.
In pursuit of virtue, I imagine. How hard a thing
is that to come by? Did my son,
belongings split between two houses,
ever find his black shoes?
Come with me, sneak downstairs, they won't notice
two grownups in jeans and sweaters.

The sun on April 18 hangs late in the sky
for the first time in seven months
as if someone turned up the heat.
Bombs are falling in Kosovo,
poets struggle to separate the impure
from the pure, but these kids, oh these kids:
their priorities are clear.

Wildlife on Old Wood Road

Six a.m., returning home at first light,
my headlamp startles a white ptarmigan.
It flies up from the edge of the road
to hide in the aspen tops, black tail wings a shock.
Silent and fast it transforms from a fat bird
to triangular fighter. A moose appears
huge, silent and complete
against the trees. Two calves with her, giant teenagers.
Her ribs press against the brown suitcase of her hide.
She looks exhausted.

This morning my eyes are filling with tears.
I'm back in my mother's last year,
I'd like to do it over, I'd like
to be there again.
A fox separates from the snow uphill
orange fur fluffed out for warmth
slips down the road and into the woods.
Solitary, even though head of a household.
She was that way—she never once complained
of the solitude, or the silence.

Is it wrong to see the world of the animals
intersect with mine, to see boundaries
unfixed? All things brush one another,
have the power to astonish, adjust,
even comfort. I return to my cave,
my sleepy mate upstairs.
He could teach a cat
to relax. The comforts of my nest
pull me back to this hour, though it mixes
with the next.

The Light that Fills the World

In the high arctic where the sun
and the atmosphere are the only painters,
touching and highlighting edges and drifts,
and to survive the night is a gift
poets sang this song:
"there is only one great thing,
the only thing:
to live to see in huts
and on journeys
the great day that dawns,
and the light that fills the world."

This winter morning in Fairbanks
I waited outside my son's school
A Diamond taxi slid up to the curb
pink kayak in the ice fog.
A boy climbed out
bare arms, no jacket
no books. And no lunch.
There are different ways of having nothing.

I think, for the man or woman who looks after him
daylight came too soon.
I too have been held to my bed mornings
And yet I was wanted, loved, in the scheme of things.
Light that brings news of the day
also brings promise, at last brought me yours.
I will not forget you, ever, you said,
and those words alone
healed me.

Boletus

"Earth and the great weather
...move my inward parts with joy."
  —Osarqaq (translated from the Inupiaq by Knud Rasmussen)

Out of a paper cup
from which a forget-me-not
or some other northern flower
was to have sprung
rises a boletus
on a trunk the size
of a man's thumb.
What a surprise,
nosing aside the petals
of a nasturtium, this meaty umbrella.

Boletus, how did we come
by you? Did spore
float this way on the breeze
or was it in the soil
which I scooped into pots
to prettify this deck
You tip forward
From a little cup
intended for lemonade. Tennyson,
struck by a flower
in the crannied wall
sang to it then plucked it out
as if paying a compliment.

You're not
the plucksome sort.
You wouldn't last long
out of the earth
despite this need to burst
through unresisting air
I could slice and fry you for breakfast

or leave you be
where you move my inward parts with joy.
You're a softy, boletus,
but you've got me.

And the Bridegroom

(On the painting by Lucian Freud)

A black screen between the bed and the window
gives them privacy, the quantity of sheet
spilled on the floor is like a wedding train.
Look at his torso huge in sleep,
legs like a Percheron's, body without shame.
She's curled next to him, fetal, white,
a marionette of bones. Her stomach droops
from a once-youthful cage.
Human, she is human again
immortality rising and falling
in her breath. They brought to this bed
darkness and light both:
The white light of the painter's vision,
the all-absorbing black screen,

and this new light
that rises from their sleep.
Her ankle rests atop his calf. The knife
used to paint his legs and chest
gloried in long strokes, while it dipped
and pulled the ends of all her bones.
He's toast-colored, she's water-lily pale
warm in the shadow near his skin
her knees and hips and shoulders
a sharp and trembling arrangement
you know was taken not long before
without complaint into the heat
of his coming, flowers burst
and blooming, while behind her eyelids
one greeting filled the whole world.

Easter Breakfast

I wander down for breakfast to find
rhapsody, a man in the kitchen
in a green t-shirt, wild nests in his black hair
from the pillow he's recently left
forearms by Michelangelo reaching for a frying pan
a grin on his face, because it's Easter
and I'm watching him, dancing now as he lays
slices of ham in the pan, cracks open eggs.
Redpolls are at the feeder, old snow pockmarked
with spruce seeds, the house is perched like the prow
of a kayak on the steep hillside. Today the hill
is a wave, we've arrived on the crest, and the day itself,
the year ahead, are the tipsy, dangerous Sound
that will send us into a new life,
after breakfast.

Knowing Full Well What We Long For

My hands meet the shape of your face
I am stunned as the years
drop from you

desire
that word alone among all others
no matter what is done to it
that survives each generation
gleaming

Light and Its Absence

1.
Flames in dark glass flicker
at the entrance to a side chapel.
Banks of candles in black iron frames,
black and red. Lit and unlit. I am ten years old.

Below the candles a dark board
on which to knot my hands and examine
any troubling secret, which will rise
in the darkness, offer itself

for judgment or mercy under the gaze
of an olive-eyed saint. Everywhere carvings
like footnotes in stone.
They left no surface unworked in the old days.

I stare at the bowed backs of men and women
praying in the shadows at the feet of saints
whose white faces, like wandering rocks,
shine only with reflected glory.

2.
In a blazing new parish in Fairbanks, Alaska,
the one great room is white with light.
It could be a dentist's office; globes like snowballs
press on my eyes, threaten to conquer sin with wattage.

My son pounds a keyboard
and teenage girls with a gap of pink
above their low-slung waistbands
send up sweet voices in counterpoint

to the winter solstice: *sun, sun, sun, here it comes.*
At the kiss of peace we gladhand each other like doctors
at a conference. There is no place to kneel
but at communion the priest smiles and says my name

as if he is glad to see me. *Thanks be to God*
and folding chairs return to their closet. We are sprung
into darkness and the lingering moon.
A halogen lamp near the sidewalk
illuminates a birch tree, whose frosted branches
weave a basket above our heads against the night.

Coming Up On Solstice

For one month a thin dry crust of snow
grew even thinner in the woods.
I almost mailordered a snowglobe
just to dream on fresh snow again.
This morning, what a blessing.
It fell all morning and kept on
while I prepared the meals, whipped my inbox
into shape. At three we set out for the post office
a two-mile walk, down the road.

I thought I knew softness
—silk, petals, that white fur
on the cat's throat, your body
underneath our quilt—
but this softness blended
substance into air.
Twelve miles to the north
downtown Fairbanks blinked at us
The lights of a plane coming our way
made a starry cross in the sky
and hovered like a Christmas card.

We walked from this view into the woods
as if into a Basho print, where limbs of birch trees
were black stripes under corresponding loads of snow.
I said, suffused with the moment
of creation, "It seems
as if there are no shadows!"
Limping behind on a recently torn knee
you said, "That's because there are none.
You need the sun or moon for shadows."
All we had was the faintest wash
of grayish violet in half the sky, and by the time
we climbed back up the hill

that, too, was gone. Inside my backpack
Christmas catalogs blazed like flashlights
left on in a dark room.
We lost the tracks we had been following,
and waded home in the dark
across the unplowed land.

Non

A spot on the map, Nondalton, Alaska, intrigues
with its certainty. Whatever else this place is,
Dalton it's not. Slide this hollow, holy sound
up against a noun: and voila, appears a thing
you'd never considered. Euclideans and smokers,
meet your counterparts. Propped against violence
(like two passengers on a Greyhound bus)
the road to despair becomes a sunlit highway.
More brave and beautiful a concept never existed.
Slice it away to reveal chalant and warm with me
to possibility when, alas, too soon arrives
Shakespeare's man in tunic, tights and curly shoes
to strum a lute and call us from this nonsense with a hey
nonny nonny there are other subjects for poetry:
God, and his absence. Love, and the longing for.

Note: The place name Nondalton, also known as Nuvendalton, is a
corruption of Noondalty, from the Tanaina Indian language, and has
nothing to do with the subject of this poem.

Travel

Inside, Outside, Morningside

Falling snow caps the rails
of the *MV Epiphany*.
The silent, heavy water tolerates us well.
We're going outside on the Inside Passage, a journey
crowded with ghosts.
They pile up like the snowfall on the gangway—
my madness for you,
the dead suddenly with me again,
the forsaken, his book in the ferry's gift shop,
and your past, that younger man
with black sideburns I've seen in pictures.

"There are people walking around Fairbanks
who are locked in prisons of one kind or another,"
I wrote years ago, reviewing a book of jailhouse poetry.
Then I hauled that epiphany off the pretty page
back into my heart
where the truth of it lay sleeping.
Something I've gained using words this way—
I mean incompletely understood, but every day—
is distance.

A seiner works parallel to us in the mist.
A fisherman on his own. It's been the same
for one hundred years in Alaska. You can't set foot
on a boat or plane without choking on dreams,
unrealized ones, glorious ones, private dreams.
White on white on the painted rails,
diluting the grey water, falling snow
is superfluous, an artist's privilege.
Dreams are thick
even if locked tight in every heart.

Open a wrist to let them out
and it would have meant Morningside for you.
Distance is the thing, "for fellows whom it hurts to think."

And it always hurts, this moving about, remembering,
these dreams that inhabit us like ghosts.
The conscience is troubled, says Wait,
Wait. Every human cry of horror
dissolves into the wet air.
It's been twenty years or more
since my last boat ride.
The route shudders and tips. I carry my ghosts
and you carry yours, everywhere we go—
Inside, Outside, Morningside.

*Note on the title: This is an old expression from Alaska's territorial
years: "Inside" referred to Alaska, "Outside" to everywhere else, and
"Morningside" to the hospital in Oregon that received Alaska's mentally
ill.*

Sean MacDiarmuid's Cottage

I remember the day at Kiltyclogher,
Ruined cabins among the blackberries.
The father and son, shabby as unemployed Alaskans,
who took it on themselves to give a tour.
Our son Desmond, not yet two—
Sean MacDiarmuid's cousin—
climbed the stone wall with a fistful of pebbles.

In the cottage a letter on display:
I have never been so happy
and at peace, he wrote,
the day before his execution.
In the village his statue, a small graceful man
on a ludicrous pedestal.
Like you, much loved.
He charmed his cousin Brigid
your grandmother, teasing her
like a trout to the surface.
Later he went to Dublin and martyrdom
and she went to America.
Twenty years old, cleaning Madison Square Garden,
she saved a hockey puck for you
decades before you were born.

Soon enough, there you were,
black hair like waves breaking
and hazel eyes. Lovers, we played at war.
I held your hips
between my legs. You could not fight back
and laugh at once.
We were happy, I believe we were
with our own young children in 1992
wandering through Leitrim and Kiltyclogher
looking for them—Brigid and Sean—
teenagers gone off to different wars.

On a Photograph in *The Irish Times* of a Mother and Daughter in Kashmir

Her tunneled cheek and ruined eye
gored with acid on her way to school.
Wimpled in gauze she poses with her mother,
who smiles at the photographer
because her daughter is alive.
To love a child is to see
the running toddler, the schoolgirl,
the young woman of last week
in this scarred and swaddled figure.

Walking between ancient walls
on Inis Meáin, I rest my hand
against a stone. Without mortar
these connect one to one
across the whole of Ireland.
Like words, too, set against each other
for good or ill.
I would like to build an explanation,
but cannot. Her crime was to be a woman
leaving her head unveiled.
At sixteen she woke to a life sentence.

These walls have held for centuries.
They are not likely to fall upon me now
breaking the soft skin, crushing the heart
putting an end to criminal ways.
And yet, improvising as we must,
so often we misspeak,
set disaster in motion
when words like stones are placed
between us, to build
a wall or road or arsenal
across the holy, sweet, familiar ground of human life.

Women's Christmas, Glenstal Abbey

Eight of us in the congregation, widely spaced
in the pews on January 6, keep our coats on.
It's not often that I see my breath in church.
Thirty monks in white wool robes, joined today by nuns
in blazers, make a half circle at the altar.

"If you want to," said the leper, "You can cure me."
"Of course I want to," said Jesus.

Where else have I been in a church this cold
with this same tang of life—not spruce boughs, holly, candles,
but yeast and hops. The Rainier Brewery, in Seattle.
Playing tourist in our home town
with my sister, before I knew I carried
the family illness. At the end of the tour
I could drink, safely, one glass of beer chilled to 38 degrees.

Or you could cure me.
I want you to.

Hunger and thirst lead us forward. The abbot,
warm in his robe, offers bread, as though
he knows me. I turn short, dismiss the wine,
remembering even so the temple in south Seattle
under the red R, where floors are washed every thirty minutes,
a day trip years ago in good company
before I began the longer journey
that finds me here in Ireland for *Nollaig na mBan*,
the Women's Christmas. Thinking of my sister,
my mother, how what we accept
shapes us, may at last find us willing
to be healed.

Reversal in Sligo

Hunting fuel for the frigid cabin
we drove at twilight into spruce trees
that cover the slope of Ben Bulben like a punk haircut.
The margin of the track crumbled beneath us.
Turns out the road was made of lace.
Huge rocks, only mud and sand
to hold them in place, under a thin cover of tar.
December's light fading fast, a page of music
when there's no stopping it. The mountain
and the trees turning black.

"What would you be doing on this road?"
Once off his tractor the small dark man
in a slicker never met my eyes.
"Watching Ben Bulben," I lied. Better to play tourist
than admit to scavenging firewood
from the Board of Forestry. His bare hands
parted a stone from the roadbed,
grasped another, wrestled them into place.
With hands alone he rebuilt the margin
while the Toyota hung above him.
"Try that now."

and put his shoulder to the bonnet
as the wheel found its grip,
backed over the new bridge.
Even then no exchange of names.
"Will you take something for a pint?"
Running back to his tractor:
"I do not take the pint."
Free of all that.
Hands alone he offered us
that knew their way around a stone.

Apple Wood

for Marie

Apple wood burns hot in the outdoor fireplace.
Today we twisted red and golden fruit
from the trees in your orchard,
hosed away the dust and pesticide.
We'll fly home with our treasure
rinsed and wrapped and boxed, leaving you

to an empty house. You'll lock the doors,
climb the spiral staircase
to sleep alone in the king-sized bed.
Your family is scattered, its cables frayed
as if you are riding a ghost ship strung
with tattered flags, visited by the owl in the pines.

Husband and sons left, not to abandon you
but to flee their own darkness. You waken
to empty rooms, the owls, the whisper
of the automatic sprinkler as fruit ripens
in the well-watered desert
At night you select wood from the heap of pruned branches
and build a fire, coals
warming the air when you climb from the pool.

Your routine serves an empty house.
You made a home once for me. Now I pray that you
will find reason to walk away from here,
this duty wrung out.
Families have their triumph and their end.
Unknown to me
your many seasons of harvest,
color filling the hand,
clean tart flavor at the core.

Rattlesnake Country

Knee deep in balsamroot and lupine
we wade the crest of Umtanum Ridge
as the balm of May rolls over us.
A motorboat carves a wake
in the still water above the dam.

At a grassy shelf
water drips from a pipe
into a galvanized trough.
Marie points out tadpoles, limbs emerging
like those magnetized fish with legs
noncreationists fix to their cars
as if to say, Salvation may be a fish to you
but Christ was a human being like me
and our story on earth
is longer than six days, ten thousand years,
longer than the hardest times
endured by a hundred thousand women marching,
sitting by wells, brushing away flies,
enduring the loss
of their children.

Today is Mother's Day. Our sons live elsewhere
and we wonder separately what they are doing.
We leave this resting place of green
that a trickle of water makes possible.
Because it is spring, snakes take to the path to bask.
A rattle at my ankles and I shoot up inside my boots.
Marie reaches forward and pulls me away.
Here's what I like about rattlers:
they don't come after you.
Someday, I announce, I'm going to keep walking
for a thousand miles, two thousand.
Won't carry a backpack.
Just for the thrill of it, fling out my legs
across this landscape. Why should I stop?
You come, too.

Sugar in the Universe

Flown in from Idaho when the local harvest failed,
two pounds of Bing cherries from this plywood shack
appear to be all mine. My fingertips turn black.
I'm startled when a pit goes down.
Cherries fill my entire internal canal
turning my exterior self smutty and sweet.
Dark and warm from a plastic bag
I can't count them anymore.
You thought I came here to be with you—
I came to Michigan to eat cherries,
no matter where they came from.

Thirst

Isle Royale, logged, mined, micromanaged
by the park service, a green laboratory
more than a wilderness, wrung us dry
after days of hiking. We boil and sip
the animal-rich water, follow loons
and otters in the cove. A pleasure boat moors
and laughter swirls up as if from a parking lot.

Four young men clean and grill their trout.
Exhausted on my rock I watch an ant drag a caterpillar
past me, fight off another for the prize.
Smoky warm water in plastic canteens
down by half. We are drawn into ourselves
from thirst. Suddenly on a ridge, the blueberries.
We sink into them like bears
drop backpacks, fall to consuming. Gather a handful,

palm them in. Burst of pure, wild sweetness.
Too many all around, not enough inside.
Late in the day we walk into raspberries;
stickers scratch bare legs as we feast
hand to mouth. "Look up," says Pat, "how they go on."
Where did this greed come from, is it only imbalance?
As with the earth island, so with you and me?

When at last we soldier on, asters wink on every side,
petaled lanterns glowing us toward camp.

An Alaskan in Claremont

After a morning in the theological library, I walk
into the mild breeze, stepping over olives
fallen from overburdened trees. Thyme and lavender

flower in a dry yard. Rows of orange trees
guide me to a wall where camellias bloom
round and solid as balls of ice cream. My eyes

are dazzled by what leaps from the ground in California:
spears of yucca forming perfect half-domes
puckerish oranges never destined for Safeway

these white camellias. "They don't tolerate water,"
my sister tells me, "a drop of water on the petals,
and they turn brown." Such a world

that has these shapes in it, colors exploding
not from a paint box but from the earth.
Behind the dormitory are lime and lemon trees;

a thieving hand shoots up. I pass a shrub of pointed,
dark green leaves. Did you know that bay laurel
comes this way, lush and soft, not pale and crisp

in a plastic box? Not rubbish to be lifted out of pasta
but greenery to make a wreath. They call this climate
Mediterranean, after the one that nourished the religion

of my ancestors. Rugged summits separating
mild valleys, life softened with oil, herbs and wine,
rumors unstoppable mixing with labor and trade,

these images, this weather loading the psalms I crave.

Mediterranean Evening

"The affectionate air, all whisper and caresses…"
  —San Juan de la Cruz, "Spiritual Canticle"

Like exotic fish released into water
of exactly the correct degree, we surrender
to evening in Leon.
We have no word back home for this ambience.
Walk into the soft breeze and astonish your skin.
Don't pray so much, take this time to greet
one another, watch small children
tear across the plaza.
This air is what our ancestors knew.
We'll pick up the trail again in the morning. For now
be at home in this softness through which Jesus and Mary,
Suliman and Roxelana, Claudius, Hippocrates
and Homer walked in the evening. The very same.

Pilgrim Refuge, Villafranca Del Bierzo, Spain

"There is something in you that is equal to what surpasses you."
—Paul Valery

Stretched out between my son and my husband, the day's walk accomplished, my eyes are drawn to the open balcony door. The wind lifts the leaves of the tall willows and when it subsides, they relax, only to be lifted again and again in the soft air of evening, like waves against a beach. We have a room to ourselves tonight on the second floor of the Municipal Refuge in Villafranca del Bierzo. Perhaps we are missing out on a colorful evening at the funky refuge up the hill—isn't it our duty as travelers to seek out color, camaraderie, stories? Instead we have found some peace, and on this steep hillside we are at the level of the treetops that bend and sigh off the balcony. Where I come from, in Alaska, the air is rarely if ever like this—tending you so well while you stretch out, safe, relaxed, with nothing to do, windows flung open for hours at a time. Something in me is fully awake. Call it surprise, that the tired human animal fits so well on this planet. My astonishment renews itself with every breath of wind.

The Beach at Finisterre

We walked six hundred miles to get here,
one month across Spain on the Camino Francés
to the end of the land. We pay our respects
to the lighthouse, turn back, then see this beach
to the north, below a hillside of nettles,
fight our way down, pull off boots, and offer our flesh
to the Atlantic. Breakers roll forward in layers
to bathe your legs, scratched like the baroque Christ's
we saw in the village church. The scythe of white sand
is deserted but for the two of us. Sea water swirls
then ebbs, pulling grains of sand
from under soles used to pounding the ground.

So much like home that I am home,
back on the Olympic Peninsula in Washington State.
God's child in Coconut Grove and nothing matters.
We walk back and forth entranced
by this prayer that children all over the world
perform on a beach, again and again. Front the water's
icy tongue, retreat. The murmur of surf
is like the din of a Wednesday rosary
in a Spanish cathedral, or that chanting
I investigated at midnight in the pilgrim hostel
to find a young man reviewing his stock quotes
on a cell phone. Sacred and profane honor each other,
the music I love best playing in Galicia.

Old Clothes

Piled sky high in the alley behind the thrift shop
colors fading like a field
that is tired of the plow
Sweaters dull shirts pajamas
soft as hundred-thousand lire notes.
Later today a pair of hands
will shake out every wrinkled top
pleats beyond salvation, pirated Izods
these odd checkered pants.
Give each a price

This Seminoles t-shirt
may end up on a boy with a chalky face
hawking one pocket pack of Kleenex
to a tourist outside Saint Anthony's church in Istanbul
over the shirt a blazer
meant for someone twice his size
old clothes are not poetry

but closer to prose,
like some cart or wheelbarrow
retrieved from a yard, we can make use of this,
or a raft we've built to ride out
the hard times. But how they travel,
these shirts and sweaters, how they
link us like some loosely knitted version
of brotherhood.

Dutch Interiors

Alternating tiles of black and white,
an open half door, the wind-eye beyond.
Nor were they wrong, the old masters,
about the revelations of Dutch interiors.
As we pedal along the canal I take in
grand pianos, sculpture, table set for dinner,
that wall of books,
a woman chasing a child through the room.
Second nature to provide a feast
to the passing stranger's glance.
This little nation
turns lack of space to an advantage.
As if to say,
you're so close, why not look inside?

Tonight the woman you planned to marry
thirty-five years ago meets us at an outdoor cafe.
Her smile instantly familiar to me from photographs,
she leaps to take your hands,
announces "three times in Holland"
and kisses your face—
right, left, right again,
speaks your name over and over,
produces the same pictures
I've seen at home: the two of you in Mexico,
against a rented Cessna
(*Did he ever take you flying?* she asks me)
her bare legs curled
around the branch of a tree
as she hangs upside down in a bikini
on the lakeshore in Michigan.

Despite the clanging of this Amsterdam square,
the talk and bicycle bells,
she hears a noise inside her purse
digs for a cellphone, reads the tiny screen with a laugh:

"It's my neighbor,
Asking *how is he? After all this time?*"
Like you so nervous beforehand
to awaken ghosts, allow memory in
to undercut the surface
of her life. She's brought grown sons
along to reassure us all. But *"Look at you,"* she says
of the slim darkhaired pilot
in her wallet of photos.
The wind-eye is open.
We gaze with human envy
on the two of you together
in obvious tenderness
and lust. Like a passerby encouraged
by this half door ajar
I am treated to the youth of the man I love.

A Heart that is Pleased by the Sea

Singers in blouses of gold and red beam at the late arrivals
beckon us inside. Eight centuries
of supplication and dread
have polished the interior of St. Magnus Cathedral to a dull rose.
Carved skulls at eye level so alike and unlike each other
you know the sculptor was toying with his formula
as he gouged the sockets a little too deep
tilted the chin a little too far.

I'm not afraid of bones but this vaulting space, these tombs
have me tightening my arms around my chest.
A young man steps forward, his own skull gleaming
and lifts a solitary voice: *It was there that we parted*
In yon shady glen, on the steep steep sides of Ben Lomond...
Against the reprimand of eternity
his story of heartbreak is the assurance of love.

One afternoon we come to Skipi Geo,
a cut in the land where fishermen pulled up from the sea.
We climb onto flagstones the color of peat to meet an undiluted blue.
The wild shout of meeting is tossed high above us.
When the waves draw back a pile of foam turns yellow on the rock.
You can't get your fill, turn to me at last:
"What are you thinking?" Like a sailor

tacking through the wind toward a beloved shore.
What masquerades as a question
comes to me a promise: in my joy I turn to you.
So broken are my thoughts in the wind
I can't find a sentence to save my life.
Only this: what would keep us apart,
this wind, this spinning globe, brings us together,
two hearts pleased by the sea.

Orkney Lace

For all their bloody history, the islands
lie suntoasted, rounded, mild
in the North Atlantic, surrounded by Orkney lace:
seafoam. A land the color of biscuits.
But here at the broken cliffs of Skipi Geo
we find pigment raw from the tubes.
Things of man meet a wild negation.
Arguments I bring from home snap and fly away.
I have lost everything,
all the things I carry.
Let me always live by the sea.

Water

"What do you think," I whispered,
Is the traditional gift for a sixth anniversary?
You whispered back,
"Water."

One August day,
Canadian kids back in school,
our two kayaks skated alone
over water deep and cold and absolutely still,
as if Lake Superior were meditating on its own clarity.
We ran the boats up onto a boulder
and bare skin met warm granite
until helicopters filming a Park Service video
chased two lovers from a private world.

On a flooded gravel pit back home in Fairbanks
I paddled a craft that you created
from plywood, glue and stitches,
turned over to me for its maiden voyage.
Go ahead, you said, and with those words
gave me that still brown pond,
filled with upside down trees
and secret places where ducks nested behind the willows.

On a lakeshore in Michigan.
I watch a family of mergansers ride up
and down the waves, and suddenly,
I remember rivers. The Chena slowing after her ride through the hills,
undercutting the bank, dropping spruce
whole into the current,
the Nenana roaring past the carcass of a whale
who missed her turn out in Norton Sound
and Tolovana Creek cooling the hot springs,
inviting with steam
the wicked, the loose, the courting, the lost.

Years ago, we flung ourselves forward on skis
over windy, bald summits, carrying
gear enough to keep us alive at twenty below zero
eleven miles to reach that valley
where hot water rises
from a fault in the earth's crust.
When we climbed in, comet Hale-Boggs
was plastered on the night sky
and a ring of cedar planks
held us red and steaming, coopered together
in the stream.

The work of our hands

A Poem in the Hand: Not Drinking Song

Like a piece of ice on a hot stove a poem should ride on its own melting.
  —Robert Frost.

No no no no, I don't drink it no more
  —Hoyt Axton

A poem in the hand is not like a bird
stunned in a fall, or this bottle of gin
that fits so well between my wallet
and my sunglasses in the cave of my purse.

Things that fit so well
can be well and beautifully directed,
take for example the one thing that happens to ice
on a hot stove. Or a tennis ball

or a creamy red pear or the perfect skull
of this cat. I drop my rosary
in a slow fall of beads onto the dresser top
enjoy its strange familiarity

as I would the flavor of ripening pear
turning red in the bowl
and also the cat's indifference, danger
in a bottle of gin but no no no no

I don't take it no more nor this handful
of pale blue beads which brings me the stuff
of my grandmother's living room in 1952
my father smiling on the couch just home

from a night of jazz and martinis downtown
these things would fill out a poem
and most of all this living bird
with bright eyes and tiny shocky breast

which fell from the sky onto my road
one winter day. I carried it alive
to the berm of snow, grateful
thinking, I can use this.

Henry's Nelson Coat

"She went forward impulsively, with arms outstretched. It was the beginning of the great romance that was to link their names together for all time."
—Frank Humphris, *Nelson*

This tiny blue biography of a diminutive, one-armed, one-eyed imperialist has fascinated you for years. At the age of ten you own a book you have literally read the cover off. Is it the ships? The swordplay? The language: "England expects that every man shall do his duty"? Is it the diagrams of Trafalgar? The boy Nelson swinging his musket at a polar bear? Surely it's not Lady Hamilton in her empire-waist, shawl dropping from white arms, stepping forward to meet the shy hero with the scar on his cheek and the sleeve pinned to his jacket—

We made a coat together one Halloween. I hadn't sewn in years. Every night for a week we pinned and trimmed and sewed royal blue fleece into shape. We forgot to go to Cub Scouts.

The first time you tried it on I was trembling inside. It fit to perfection. You were small and thin, but your eyes were blue, your shoulders straight, your smile that of someone who will survive many hardships, intact and spirited.

I engineered epaulets out of gold felt and gold fringe. You picked out buttons and gold braid. The coat was finished. Halloween night you carried a sword and wore medals, a black felt hat with a white plume stapled to it, and your snow boots.

For Christmas that year I bought you a royal blue bathrobe. I wasn't finished with our adventure. At the sight of you home from the wars of fifth grade, I am pulled out of everything I know.

The Top of the World From Inside Jeanie's Parka

Never have I seen the shape of the planet
until now, standing at the perimeter of this frozen ocean.
Arrested in midcurl, arctic ice is tidied up
where it meets the horizon, becomes the perfect edge
of a coin. From boxy houses villagers tumble out
to retrieve children, rent a movie, then disappear inside.
The sun, another coin, slips away by degrees
into someone else's bank. No trash whirls along the street.
Only my cheek, burning, tells me wind
moves always off that ice, and a vertical line of pure cold
penetrates the steel zipper of a handsewn parka
that weighs ten pounds and falls below my knees.
Even that is not enough when you look at the world
from the edge of the Chukchi Sea.

If You Want A Drunkard

Six camel-hide puppets, characters
from Turkish folklore. Choose one,
I told the third-grade poets.
Be a poor man carrying burdens,
a tea seller, a drunkard with jointed knees
(knife in one hand, bottle in the other),
a drummer, a musician.

Jesse was the first to read.
I am a drunkard
he announced. I am going to hell.
If you want a drunkard,
that's where I'll be.
Now how did he learn so much
about unrepentance in a Catholic school,
the glee of Paradise Lost?
What a grin. We hadn't gone around the room
before he waved his hand to ask
can I read my poem again?

Lighthouse Keeping

"Come down and redeem us from virtue…"
  —A.C. Swinburne, "Dolores"

She said to me, "I answered an ad
for lighthouse keeping."
She is a gregarious woman; yet
wouldn't the lonely posting be grand for her
or for me. Spray booming in the holes.
Perhaps the ex-prime minister with mob connections
would founder in his yacht below me
if I kept the light at Mizen Head.
I'd watch lobstermen ride the mountainous waves
compare live birds to the ones on the chart
wait for you.

Reading a book on the craft
of novel writing I come to the chapter on plot
my nemesis, because Christ
I don't know what's happening before it happens
any more than you do.
"Make a scone of it."
That I can do! Leap for the easy magic of the kitchen
where a fingertip of soda makes bread rise, gives off the scent
of heaven.

In a row of cookbooks the strange title
"Cooking Without Faith." Can that be done?
In my storm-toss't lighthouse
no company but a vibrator and a crate
labeled "Carnegie Library Lighthouse Service"
(they never send the smut I'm craving
but thank God for all this Conrad)
I put together meals for myself alone.
Spoon up my soup in the wonder and pointlessness
of solitude.

What can I do but swear that your love comes to me
with every breaking wave?
When surf fills the arch below and spray rises to the window,
it's another hymn of praise to the day
such as a man sings while shaving
before he serves breakfast to the woman
with her head in *The New York Times*,
eating the news of the universe.

Colleen Lake, Deadhorse, Alaska

Gravel roads lead past tin warehouses, generations
of derricks on their sides, earthmovers
with outsize tires like herds of thirsty elephants

I drop off the road and step across the tundra
around fox shit, foam cups, crumpled packs
of Camels, arrive to my surprise at a lake.

Long before drillers floated a gravel raft
over the tundra, Colleen Lake reflected the sky,
called to birds, come rest and eat.

No cathedrals, no monuments, no libraries
in Deadhorse, no Elks Lodge
or Lions Den. But water at the center

to lure a bufflehead and ducklings on Labor Day.
My son is building an airstrip, sent me pictures
of caribou blocking the dozers

but what is here to connect him
with his fellow creatures, to build community
except these gravel roads which keep them above the soft land

and Colleen Lake. Guessing by the trash around me,
this cold, clear mirror draws everyone at last
to stare and wonder at the place they're in.

Fire-Filled Summer

Ignited by thousands of lightning strikes
fires roared to life in the black spruce,
two, three, five at once, and dry winds
sent us smoke. The sky turned gray,
then yellow. Masked citizens
ran only essential errands
through air the color of dirty cat's fur.
A coating of ash appeared
on the car, the laundry, newly painted sills.

We woke each day to quiet and stillness,
the smell of war around us but no war,
no bombs, no screams, little traffic.
Drivers looked thoughtful, peering ahead
down roads no longer familiar,
hung with thick, rank curtains
and something called the sun grew in size,
changed color, moved in and out of haze.

Summers used to fly past: gardening at midnight,
building greenhouses, adding on. Not this year.
Six million acres blackened by summer's end.
We wandered through a changed universe
while firefighters tried to follow orders and save cabins,
burnt their feet walking on ash,
and curled up like kindergartners
for a nap in the firebreaks.

Firemoss

From the hill a blaze roared down in black spruce canopy.
Firefighters set another to combat the first.
It dove underneath, scorched the ground
took out all that was left.
Two fires colliding turned these gentle slopes
into black pan.

Three years later over the scorch appears
an emerald zone, millions of green stars.
Firemoss, glowing weirdly in the mist.
I sink my fingers deep, uproot a chunk,
it's as if I'm holding hundreds of tiny trees
in each square inch. What's underneath?
Hard, cold, black.
Small birch saplings
rise above the Technicolor bed.

The landscape hits a place in my brain
I don't like to visit, that place
where we come awake
after the battle and the rapes
to see what's been left to us,
how it is different now. This is
not the human story
but its aftermath. What we need
to turn this around is Prometheus again,
our own creative spirit
unbound.

The Dog at the Top of the Road

No more nosing for a headrub
her long blonde muzzle between my knees,
her confusion at the head of the stairs
(who goes down first? I always forget!)
No more her doe-ish leap over the hassock
at the promise of a walk.
No more her leaping out of the woods into our legs
as if to say, "Aren't we having fun?
Hey, thanks for this!"
No more returning from errands
to her silhouette in the driver's-side-window,
square head and ears like a gull-winged plane.
No more her low-bellied crawl
from a scrap of chewed underwear,
her sneezing fits next to my pillow
in the morning, her silent witness.
to the preparation of every meal
and scratch of toenails on the floor
if I dropped so much as a carrot peel
into her dish.

Star of the Animal Shelter five years ago,
she looked out at us from the newspaper
ready for new beginnings. With a sweet face
and a few dog tricks she carved out a second chance
for herself. The terror of Old Wood Road
behaved well enough when it counted.
Shenzy's second family concurs in this:
The daily nuisance of the dog's care
will be sorely missed.

Pushkin

The old cat sleeps
in the newly arrived sun. One more spring
has come his way
dropping a solar bath
on failing kidneys, old cat bones.
I check for the rise and fall of breath.

Once he stalked hares
across the yard, tracked down
chicken hearts with split-lentil eyes.
Fearless, disinterested, a poseur, a demideity.
He and the dog are strangers still
after years of eating side by side.

I remember times of wailing
into my couch, alone
and utterly baffled by life,
when suddenly a cat
would be sitting on my head.

Last week I pulled him snarling
from under a chair in Dr. Bacon's office,
held him while she examined his dull coat,
felt his ribs. Pressed where it hurt.
Eight pounds of fur and bone and mad as hell
but "He's certainly less anxious in your lap,"
she murmured, astonishing me.
I had no idea. Old cat, old friend,
have I reached some place inside,
added to your life
as you have to mine?

Last at the Gate

Prolonging this strange goodbye
unaccompanied minors and their parents
stand apart from other travelers.
You know what I'm feeling.
A twelve-year-old boy, big enough
to be expected to be tough, crumples
and weeps while his dad has to act
like it's all going to be okay.
Stay on the positive side, behave
better than we ever did as husbands
and wives. Can't let it show, this tearing inside,
this *you asked for it* heartbreak.

Batman Next Door

The old woman in pink long johns
and red flannel nightshirt
put a trembling hand on the bed
pushed herself upright
swung pink-clad, stick-like
legs over the edge and looked
at Batman. The sturdy caped figure,
hair in damp spikes from his bath,
repeated his question.
Want your light off, Gram?
Fragile, barely there, she smiled
with a fully vigorous astonishment.
I knew then she would be safe
all through the night,
with Batman in the next room.

Codladh Sámh

I climb over the rails of your hospital bed
slide down next to you. The way your face relaxes
the pressure of your bones, are all you have left to give.

Winter sunlight off a quilt of snow
fills the room. You are serene with a grown child
against you. "Side by each," you used to say. No secrets,

no life but this. When our eyes meet, love
is exchanged, without words that make sense.
Mother, you and I have become two women

doing other things, our love is like
pushing a cradle with a foot as you work
at your desk, pay the bills, write the poems

Call softly as a bird, sleep well. Codladh sámh.
Sweet dreams. Your own dreams, your own sleep.
I won't be living in your shadow any more

Time to move out in front of my life
to be exposed to light rising off the snow.
So much tyranny in this world. And one lullaby.

My love a warmth against you now, yours with me
a diamond for the two of us. Replacing all that came before.
The nights alone you handed me, the rudeness I returned.

Accepted in the pressure of our bones, knowledge
that we are loved, even though known.

Mom and her Girlfriends, Miami Beach

Cleaning out her study we could only guess
at the importance of things: a Safeway bag
holding an accrual of missals,
the oldest fallen apart.
Saint Joseph the Worker with a line of glue
around his neck. And photographs:
Miami Beach in the 1930s, before she went north
to medical school, and it all changed.
Open-toed high heels and a girl's smile,
surrounded by her Spanish bròther-in-law and his friends.
On the beach, scarved against the sun,
and a girlfriend's arms
around her bare shoulders.

The girlfriends take me by surprise.
Holding hands they walk forward
into the surf. One whose name I'll never know
has black sausage curls, a round bottom.
They twist back to grin at the photographer
showing off their swimsuits and their affection.
Here she is in riding boots, leaning against a building,
and my mom leans against her.
They look tired and satisfied
and about to start something new.

Mom had to give up girlfriends later on.
A widow with five children, a medical practice—
if she once had said, I'm not equal to this,
what would have happened to us?
They say that girls were once more affectionate
with each other.
Don't believe it. I recognize the easy tenderness, the glee,
it comes forward to my generation like a candle
traded hand to hand.
What's not to love?
Girls are like berries to spoons.

Look at my mother's face, that bliss;
look at her companion's—
ecstatic.
Holding these photographs, I know
my mother was loved. Delight came to her
in a silver dish.

When she boarded the train in 1940
She was embraced
tightly, properly, and long.

Summer Night

It's a thrill to ferry armfuls of red rhubarb
from the garden to the kitchen on June 19.
A beetle meets me face to face on the screen door.
At ten p.m. sunlight turns the treetops yellow.
and where a soaker hose drains the rain barrel
sunlight catches the drops, sparkling
the length of black among the potatoes.
I should be low to the ground weeding but for devils incarnate
we call mosquitoes, rising to the evening air.
Leafhoppers clatter in the grass, voles risk
the curiosity of cats, and twilight stretches
with a full belly beneath the wild canvas sky.

Past midnight, the woods below those buttered treetops
are stirring with animals, wondrous with light.

Leafhoppers

They fill a universe parallel to ours, clacking
and foraging below the tips of unmown grass
like a million out of work low-level musicians.
They took over the rhubarb,
turned giant acidic leaves into swiss cheese.
In the cool of the evening, they line up
on the wooden walkway to our deck. Whatever for?
Do they think they're fighter pilots
on the *Nimitz*? Dislikeable, all skeleton and appetite,
and yet we've been together all summer long.
They don't eat the best parts, and my anklebones
don't mind being knocked. I pick them off the
cucumbers and beans. Sometimes they just let you.
Even leafhoppers give it up at the end.

Raspberry Canes Along the Fence

It took me a week or so to discover they'd gone.
Enroute to the lawn you, my beloved,
pushed a roaring mower along the fence
where last year I picked a quart
of thumb-sized berries in fruit-starved Alaska.
When you heard out of me, "Pat, did you..."
I suppose you said the husband's prayer while I turned aside
and let fall one tear for labor lost. Spilt milk
and we're on to other things. Canes

rebound and hair grows back. My doctor
predicts I'll lose my own this summer, but I am told
it comes back curly. Okay by me to be curlyheaded
when next I leap to trade a row of berries for your kiss.

Forest Floor After Rain

(for Jeanie)

Our trail leads through a riot of toppled mushrooms.
One wrinkled fellow nudged with a boot
exudes fingerpaint of kindergarten yellow.
Sponges, boletus, fried chicken fungus
clump atop each other, hedgehog mushrooms
with tops like old car seats, amanitas
tawdry as revelers the day after Mardi Gras.
All day rain is open sesame to the forest floor.

Back home, "don't sit down," you cry,
hand me a steel bowl to fill with vegetables.
We race the coming downpour through your garden
with knife and shears. Curly chard, beans, leeks,
a stalk of Brussels sprouts. Your spirit aroused
you throw in cilantro, thyme, art deco squashes.
Flavors and shapes fill my arms. Is it tears or rain
upon my face? More fruiting bodies
will spring up tonight, a free-for-all
in the forest garden, untended, rampant.
Fungi work the soil all summer long;
August rain their curtain call.

Siesta

September in Alaska; warm afternoons
are numbered. Shades of black in the garden,
tomato vines broken and knobbed
like old human limbs. A shirt hung over a post in July
has turned from blue to white.
I toe my way through weeds,
step into half a roll of chicken wire.
So much to do around the place

yet I've come inside to pull off my shirt,
climb into bed with you. Weight tangled in softness
now, arms and legs hopeless to undo.
We snore together while light that would blind a preacher
fills our bedroom window. With every sigh the aspens
shiver gold upon the lawn.

An upended bowl of sky sheds radiance
on neglected chores. One look at the calendar
and we know these days are few.
I must be looking in the wrong place, so ready
am I to bank on more, unrolled to the horizon
these easy afternoons with you.

When the Bookmobile Comes to Ester, Alaska

Compost in the village burns hotter and French syllables
flow forth, the Birdman plays and John Muir with a glance
and a shrug, invites me along for a ramble up the San Gabriels.
As we walk I think, *hey—I love nature too!*
My mouth fills with glee at a new poem
into which this Czech gal stuck so many astonishing words—
lick, and suck, coddle and chew, and she meant them too.
I am soon to be glutted with blissful distractions,
recipes, my competition in the fiction contests, this haul
of books so heavy the skinny librarian—*color of the sun*
and her eyes are green—carries the bag to my car,
being younger and stronger and no way confined to bed.
Just doin' my job, she says, and gives me a hug,
with a coddle and kiss, a pinch of feverfew.

Eight-Sided Art

An octagonal dish wooed the sky in our new backyard.
We walked around it for a year or so, then Pat stripped it down,
pondered how to extend this pattern with two by fours,
heavy old windows and doors, into the earth.

I think I would like to write a poem, or a story, and heave at it. Drops fly out
around my head like a worry cartoon. I try out lines on any captive listener,
study your eyes for a flicker of interest. As Frank O'Hara knew, artists
do things differently, or did he find out we are all the same? Some call attention,

others rotate eight-pointed stars across the field in silence.
One summer day a friend with a crane lowered the roof to windowed walls.
A table in the center and seven boxes of topsoil. Now I step inside a world
that is mild and still on an April day; lift back leaves in August

to discover cucumbers. This big abandoned dish traveled thirty feet
to become a greenhouse, to recycle power from the arctic sky.

Three Birch Trees, or Maybe Four

(for Henry and Shawna, July 2007)

Jesus said, if you turn around
from the handles of your plough
to stare at the ground
you've traveled
you won't be fit for the kingdom.
Don't look back!

On the eve
of your wedding,
we plant birch trees
outside the kitchen window.
From one bucket
grow two orangey trunks,
twisted round each other.
"What's the story?"
I ask the nurserywoman
at Plant Kingdom
on Farmer's Loop Road.
Wrapped at the base,
she tells me,
they may not be strong enough
to make it. But I've seen plenty

of intertwining birches in the wild,
lovebound saplings from the get go.
I plant them together,
three birch trees
or maybe four.
As your marriage
unfurls a new canopy
under the sun
I won't look back
but wonder and watch
these slowly growing birch trees.

The Plums Are Gone

and you are a peach. Strange and wonderful
how the words of a friend
on the occasion of joy
slip without pain down through the layers of self
to the place they're looking for.
A few sentences sink through me
to find home so deftly
like nothing else I know—
God dividing butter, perhaps
or my husband meeting me more than halfway.

Republican Sweep, 2004

On the cold morning that followed
the election, I caught a glimpse
of a spruce branch heavy with snow
as I let the dog out. The forest outside
my door seemed to be saying,
Come on in.
What a beautiful place this is.
Lots to explore. I've forgotten lately.

Lessons Learned

Lessons learned are all about what works. If I go out to the garden
on a June day, where growth explodes
almost overnight, peace is there.
Weeds are irksome but also: something to do.
My inner perfectionist long since surrendered this field.
A garden is a place to putter around in.
God, there's morphine in the puttering.

If a visitor drops by, my son or sister
or friend, or friend with her little son, there will
be familiar voices, taking me outside of myself,
filling the world with goodness the way a garden
fills it with flowers, with food.

If I keep my daily list pared, I only have to think of it
to know a bit of reassurance, a soft sure thing.
The birds you hear outside have their way of being in the world,
and I have mine. Walk, pray, take the pills on schedule,
eat five times a day, and write. Let my fingers
earn their pay, let them move
like birds, tap the imperative of travel.
Our long-legged alphabet is my flock of cranes.

How quickly I forget the most important lesson,
most incompletely learned. Move on. Solve not these problems:
Let them be, or let them wither. Get thee behind me, Satan.
This bird answers to the sky. The young are strong enough;
We can go now. Take to the air, or to the road since I don't like to fly.
Is a work in progress served by turning back?
Look once, get up, and go. A little freedom in that,
just what I need to complete this cockeyed recipe
for making it through another day's haul to the things I need to see,
the vigorous crone I yearn to be.

Ice Cream

The book of my life is open
to the page on ice cream,
the only emperor. White
as New Mexican camellias
in February. The spoon curves
into a second round ball
of vanilla with brown specks
of bean. To have
a bowl of ice cream with you
after supper, I would say
we have become fearless

together.
The blood count
trembles; haven't I always stood fast?
Yet, how white it is.
As simple as possible.
Cream, sugar, vanilla,
air,
voila! We leap to refill
these begging bowls, these beautiful
empty begging bowls.
In the leap itself is all
my faith. God put me here
to leap forward with my empty bowl,
to describe a circle
with my spoon.

The Author

Marjorie Kowalski Cole was the author of two novels, *Correcting the Landscape*, which received the 2004 Bellwether Prize for fiction and was published by HarperCollins in 2006, and *A Spell on the Water,* the publication of which is forthcoming. Her award-winning poetry and fiction have appeared in numerous journals, including *The Chattahoochee Review, Grain, Antigonish Review, Passages North, Alaska Quarterly Review, Seattle Review, Prism International, Kalliope, Cream City Review*, and *Beloit Fiction Journal*. Essays on travel and writing have appeared in *Commonweal, The Los Angeles Times, Poets and Writers*, and *National Catholic Reporter*.

Born in Boston in 1953, Cole lived in Seattle before moving to Fairbanks, Alaska, with her family in 1966. She earned an M.A. in English from the University of Alaska Fairbanks and an M.L.S. from the University of Washington. She taught English, poetry, and library science and worked as a reference librarian. Always engaged with her community, she worked with the Literacy Council of Alaska, the Northern Alaska Environmental Center, the Alaska Peace Center, and the Fairbanks Arts Association, among others. She was a Benedictine Oblate, and founded Call to Action Alaska. She loved music and learned to play the banjo with Robin Dale Ford.

She married Pat Lambert in 2000, and had two sons, Henry Cole and Desmond Cole. She died in late 2009, shortly before this collection was sent to the printer.